Y0-AKU-858

The Indian in American History

Third Edition, Revised

WILLIAM T. HAGAN

240 AHA PAMPHLETS
AMERICAN HISTORICAL ASSOCIATION
400 A Street, SE, Washington, D.C. 20003

WILLIAM T. HAGAN is Distinguished Professor of History at the State University College at Fredonia, New York. He received his BA from Marshall University, served in World War II, and then enrolled in the PhD program at the University of Wisconsin. His interest in American Indians began in a seminar with William B. Hesseltine, who had close ties with the State Historical Society of Wisconsin. Professor Hagan was asked to chart the route Black Hawk followed in his retreat through Wisconsin in 1832, and this investigation led to a dissertation on the Black Hawk War. Professor Hagan received his PhD in 1950, meanwhile undertaking research projects on the Chippewa for the state of Wisconsin and on the Winnebago for a private law firm. He taught at North Texas State University before moving to New York in 1965. He is a past president of both the American Society for Ethnohistory and the Western History Association. His publications include *The Sac and Fox Indians* (Norman, 1958); *American Indians* (Chicago, 1961 and 1979); *Indian Police and Judges* (New Haven, 1966; Lincoln, 1980); and *United States-Comanche Relations* (New Haven, 1976). He is currently completing a study of the early years of the Indian Rights Association.

Earlier versions of this pamphlet appeared under the same title in 1963 and 1971. Both the text and the bibliographical material of the pamphlet as printed here have been revised to incorporate the most recent developments in this subject area.

AHA Staff Editor: MAUREEN VINCENT-MORGAN

© Copyright, THE AMERICAN HISTORICAL ASSOCIATION,
1963, 1971, 1985

All rights reserved. No part of this book may be reproduced in any form without permission in writing from the publisher, except by a reviewer who wishes to quote brief passages in connection with a review written for inclusion in a magazine or newspaper. The American Historical Association does not adopt official views on any field of history and does not necessarily agree or disagree with the views expressed in this book.

Library of Congress catalog card number: 85-47507

Printed in the United States of America

77.6
H3
985

The Indian in American History

WILLIAM T. HAGAN

Interspersed in the history of the first three centuries of the American people are numerous references to the Indians. As the inhabitants of the North American continent when Jamestown was founded, they first welcomed and then resisted the whites. Obviously an important element in American history, the Indians are dealt with by every author of secondary school textbooks.

Fundamental to an understanding of Indians in American history is an appreciation of their great cultural diversity. This is a quality not readily apparent from the frequently encountered stereotype of the Indian. The fierce, war-bonneted, mounted Plains Indian usually appears in print or on the television and movie screens. By contrast, anthropologists have identified perhaps six hundred different Indian societies and well over two hundred languages for the area now included in the contiguous forty-eight states. About one hundred fifty of these languages are still spoken.

Attempts to classify the few million Indians living in North America when the white men arrived have produced several different systems. One system assigns the Indians by tribes according to the relations of their languages to major language groups such as Athapascan, Siouan, and Algonkin. These are broad categories, comparable to Romance languages in the Indo-European family. No geographical unity is implied, and in the case of the Athapascan, tribes as far north as the Yukon and as far south as northern Mexico are included. Similarly, the Algonkin category includes the Narraganset of Rhode Island as well as the Arapahoes, who are typical Plains Indians. This wide diffusion resulted from intermittent migrations from Asia to North America over extended

160248

periods of time. (Most scholars now maintain that the first Indians arrived in North America from Asia perhaps as many as thirty thousand years ago, making their way across a land bridge where the Bering Strait now lies or by crossing what then would have been at least a much smaller body of water.)

A second system classifies the Indians according to their principal source of food. Thus, the tribes of the Pacific Northwest coast are classified in the Salmon Area. Two other such categories are the Buffalo Area, whose occupants could draw on that apparently limitless mainstay of life, and the Maize Area, which includes those tribes in the eastern half of the United States.

Still another classification system emphasizes geography. With this technique the tribes in the United States are grouped under headings such as Eastern Woodland, Plains, Plateau, and Great Basin.

Divisions by culture phenomena are also utilized. One scholar lumps the Potlatch-givers in one category, using this exaggerated form of gift giving as a type of demarcation. The People of the Calumet is the heading under which are gathered the Indians of the upper Mississippi Valley, in whose ceremonies the peace pipe, or calumet, played such a significant role.[1]

For political purposes, tribal designations are generally used, but this is a technique having, at least originally, little validity. The Indians were difficult to fit into the neat categories assigned them by whites, who were accustomed to more highly centralized governments in Europe, because the tribes were very loosely knit and were usually divided into bands or villages. The individual Indian villages can perhaps be more accurately compared to the autonomous Greek city-states. Nevertheless, over two thousand tribal designations have been employed, and even today nearly three hundred tribes are recognized by the federal government and another hundred are seeking such acknowledgment.

One typical combination encountered frequently in colonial history is the Delaware. On close examination, this apparently compact unit breaks down into scores of bands designated as Delaware, who had virtually no capacity for united political or military action and sometimes spoke different dialects. By the end

[1]Ruth Murray Underhill, *Red Man's America* (Chicago, 1953), vii.

of the eighteenth century there were Delawares scattered from Canada to Spanish Louisiana.

Likewise, as applied to Indian situations, the terms *nation, confederacy, king,* and *emperor* normally had little meaning in the European sense, yet American history is full of such references. William Penn once addressed the leading Iroquois sachem as the Emperor of Canada, and the Iroquois Confederacy was commonly spoken of as if it were a tightly knit and cohesive unit. Actually, it was a loose aggregation of five tribes (Mohawk, Oneida, Cayuga, Onondaga, and Seneca), joined by a sixth (Tuscarora) in the early eighteenth century. These tribes spoke different dialects and were frequently unable to agree on anything except the benefits of peaceful relations with each other. The Powhatan Confederacy, another one mentioned by historians, probably had more cohesion. The English were obviously still thinking in European terms when they sought to cement an alliance between themselves and these Indians by the marriage of Powhatan's daughter Pocahontas to John Rolfe. King Philip's War was begun by that Wampanoag chief, but Philip hardly exercised the degree of control over the hostile Indians that the war's name would indicate. Only among a handful of Indians in the Southeast, such as the Natchez, did the rulers reign with power commensurate with that of European monarchs.

The bewildering cultural diversity and political fragmentation of the Indians, which has confused historians, rendered the Indians incapable of withstanding the pressure of the whites. Unable to unite against the intruders, the Indians even permitted themselves to be pitted against each other by rival trading groups that sought slaves, hides, and furs. When a colony went to war against a tribe, rarely was a column of troops not accompanied by its own Indian guides and auxiliaries. The Indians were also unable to stand on the sidelines and watch the whites annihilate each other. In every conflict from the colonial wars fought by the Spanish, French, and English to the American Civil War, Indians ignored racial solidarity and could be found fighting on both sides.

English generals were not as dependent on Indian aid as the French were, and the English were sometimes quite scornful of Indian methods of fighting. Compared to an English regular, the warrior was undependable. Whether or not he chose to fight on a certain day depended upon a number of factors, including how he might have interpreted recent dreams. The warrior was also not reluctant to expose a carefully laid ambush by precipitate action, if in the process he could take the first scalp or otherwise distinguish himself. To march when ordered and to fight when ordered were completely alien to his outlook. To a general like Braddock, accustomed to troops disciplined to respond to orders like automatons, Indian warriors who were individualistic to the point of anarchy might make a mob, but not an army. As irregular troops, however, Indians did have their uses. In a reference to the Iroquois, a Frenchman described the qualities that made them valuable: "They approach like foxes, fight like lions, and disappear like birds."[2]

It is not surprising that in the contest for control of North America the Indians were found more frequently on the side of the French than the English. Francis Parkman's dictum, "Spanish civilization crushed the Indian; English civilization scorned and neglected him; French civilization embraced and cherished him,"[3] has some validity. The English lust for land, which embittered their relations with the Indians, compared most unfavorably with the French concentration on the fur trade, which was of mutual benefit to the parties involved. Despite official encouragement of agriculture in Canada, to the Indian the typical Frenchman remained the trader. The French trader, who probably had an acknowledged Indian wife and a brood of mixed-blood children, brought the Indians kettles, blankets, axes, and firearms. By contrast, the typical Englishman was the settler encroaching upon Indian land and driving away the game upon which the Indian depended.

Fur trade in the English colonies, however, was not unimportant. Tribes of that area were active in the fur trade from the first contacts with the whites. The Indians were gathering furs to trade to Europeans for perhaps a century before the first permanent settlements were planted in the thirteen colonies. French traders in the 1560s were so active along the Middle Atlantic Coast that they alarmed the Spanish who were operating out of Florida.

[2]Quoted in Underhill, *Red Man's America,* 96.

[3]Francis Parkman, *The Jesuits in North America* (Boston, 1867), 1: 131.

Throughout the colonial period and well into the nineteenth century the fur trade was one of the principal business enterprises in America. Early American history records numerous inter-colonial quarrels, with each governor trying to advance the interests of his faction of traders. As long as the British permitted each colony to make its own Indian policy—and this was essentially true until the French and Indian War—these inter-colonial differences over Indian policy were inevitable.

The Indians were more than suppliers of furs. The Pilgrims in New England and Captain John Smith in Virginia profited from Indian advice and counsel in adapting to a new land. Indians introduced the settlers to tobacco and maize and helped them to locate the waterways and passes that opened up the interior. Unfortunately, in both Virginia and New England the amicable relations that characterized this early stage quickly gave way to bitterness and hostility. Claiming all the land by right of discovery, the English usually followed the practice of the Massachusetts Bay Colony and were unwilling to compensate the Indians for hunting grounds, recognizing only the Indian title to land actually occupied or cultivated. Fraud and pressure characterized many of these negotiations. The settlers were horrified and embittered by the tactics employed in warfare by the Indians, which included scalping infants and torturing captives; the whites called these actions atrocities. Numerous clashes provided ample opportunity to document this charge.

The Indians opposed the whites independently in desperate rearguard actions and allied with one European power against the other in the colonial wars. Sometimes, as in Opechancanough's uprisings in Virginia (1622 and 1644) or King Philip's War in New England (1675-76), the Indians made a last convulsive effort to stop the advance of the frontiersmen. In contrast, the Iroquois War (1684-89) and the Yamasee War (1715-16) were trade wars. The Iroquois, backed by the English, fought the French and their Indian allies for control of the fur trade. The Yamasees rose after being driven to desperation by the extortionate practices of South Carolina traders.

Dynastic rivalries far from the American scene also produced wars that took Indian lives. King William's War (1689-97), Queen Anne's War (1702-13), King George's War (1744-48), and the French and Indian War (1754-63) all saw painted warriors raiding frontier settlements and defending their own crops and villages. Indian support was absolutely essential to successful Spanish and French operations, and vital to the English. The force that ambushed General Braddock near the forks of the Ohio was predominantly Indian, and Braddock might have avoided the disaster had his force been better supplied with Indian scouts.

History has no record of the sufferings and the triumphs of the Indians except that left by white observers, which is often less than sympathetic. If the tragedies inflicted on Indian families are lost in the limbo of history, those of their white counterparts are well recorded. The captivity narrative, written by a child who survived the forced march to some Indian village or French fort, or by a widow who had been slapped in the face with her husband's scalp, was standard fare for colonial readers. Reflecting the hate and fear Indians inspired among the whites, colonial histories and sermons abounded with references to "heathen," "savages," and "infidels." The Puritan divine, Cotton Mather, was of the opinion that "probably the Devil decoyed... [them] hither, in hopes that the gospel of the Lord Jesus Christ would never come here to destroy or disturb his absolute empire over them."[4] There was little here of the myth of the noble savage found so frequently in contemporary European literature.

Historians have observed that the necessity of coping with this Indian menace forced some of the first experiments with colonial union. The confederation of New England originated in Connecticut's Indian troubles in 1643. Over a century later, colonial representatives met at Albany to try to formulate a common policy for dealing with the Iroquois. The Albany Congress did propose a plan of union drafted by Benjamin Franklin, but colonial particularism and Crown opposition prevented adoption of the plan.

A few years later, when the colonists sought their independence, most of the tribes supported George III. Issues that acerbated British-American relations had frequently found the former cast in the role of guardian of Indian interests. British plans to revamp administration of the fur trade and to regulate more closely the

[4]Quoted in A. Irving Hallowell, "The Backwash of the Frontier," in Walker D. Wyman and Clifton B. Kroeber, eds., *The Frontier in Perspective* (Madison, 1957), 231.

movement of settlers west of the Appalachians after the French and Indian War did not originate with Pontiac's Conspiracy. The British did not need that Ottawa warrior to convince them of the danger implicit in the uninhibited activities of fur traders, land speculators, and home seekers.

The action taken in the Proclamation of 1763 and subsequent measures to extend Crown influence in these areas further alienated the colonists and contributed to the final rupture. When it came, the Indian problem had outgrown strictly local interest and had become an imperial issue. Jefferson included in the Declaration of Independence charges that George III had used Indians against the frontier settlements.

The British hastened to ensure the loyalty of the Indians and employed them extensively during the war. Recognizing where their interests lay, the Indians needed little urging to ally themselves with their father, the king. Agents of Congress working among the Indians were usually happy to settle for a tribal declaration of neutrality. When this was not obtainable, punitive expeditions might be dispatched. The Cherokees suffered heavily in retaliation for their attacks on the Tennessee settlements. Raids in central New York by the disaffected Iroquois so devastated this granary of Washington's army that he suspended other operations until these Indians could be punished. Washington was unwilling, however, to divert troops to protect the remote Virginia frontier from attacks from north and west of the Ohio. Virginia itself authorized and supported George Rogers Clark's expedition into the Illinois country.

The Indians' opposition to the Americans in the Revolution ensured that Indian relations with the new government would be off to an uneasy start. It soon became apparent that the United States had simply assumed the role formerly played by the Crown in mediating between the oppressed and badgered tribesmen and the aggressive frontiersmen and traders. Only the locale changed. The tribes east of the Appalachians had been decimated or dispossessed by 1783. Their remnants were either in flight or at the mercy of the new government. Although the term *reservation* had not yet become common, the system usually associated with a later period had already been instituted. Under close surveillance, the Indians did not abandon their native culture and adopt that of their conquerors. The only Indian acquisitions were new vices like drunkenness and new diseases like measles, smallpox, and chicken pox. A governor of Carolina saw the hand of Providence in the Indian susceptibility to these diseases because, as he noted sanctimoniously, the English were by nature too kind to kill off the Indians as the Spanish had done.[5]

Between 1783 and 1840 the Americans corrupted and dispossessed a new set of tribes between the Appalachians and the Plains country. Similar in culture to those of the eastern United States, these Indians maintained permanent villages around which the women raised quantities of corn, melons, and beans. Periodically, hunting parties left the villages to harvest the furs and skins, which the Indians exchanged with the traders for goods. As the Indians became more dependent upon the traders for a wide range of commodities—guns and ammunition, kettles, blankets, hoes, knives, and mirrors, to name only a few—native crafts were forgotten. By the late eighteenth century Indians such as the Shawnee or Cherokee, if cut off from these commodities, would quickly have been at the mercy of their enemies and the elements.

The cultural diversity that had confused the whites encountering their first Indians was conspicuous in this region also. Some northern tribes—Chippewa, for example—raised very little food but gathered large quantities of wild rice to supplement their hunting. Types of Indian dwellings ranged from the bark or mat-covered wigwams in the North to the thatched huts of the South. This diversity was seldom recognized fully by administrators and lawmakers in Washington.

To cope with the Indian problem in this period the federal government developed a series of policies, many of which were obviously a product of colonial experience. The federal government had earlier arrogated to itself control of all aspects of Indian affairs, including the purchase of Indian land and the control of Indian trade. The Articles of Confederation conferred this authority through a clause devoted to the subject. The Constitution did so by reserving treaty-making power and control of commerce to the federal government. Treaties remained the means of dealing

[5]See William Christie Macleod, *The American Indian Frontier* (New York, 1928), 50. The governor was John Archdale.

with the tribes until 1871, despite the obvious absurdity of using the same techniques for negotiating with the Cherokees as with the French.

Gradually, a United States program for the Indians began to emerge. Through a series of trade and intercourse laws, regulations were laid down for defining Indian country and controlling the contacts between Indians and whites. Agents were appointed for the principal tribes, and these agents in turn were grouped under superintendents, like William Clark at St. Louis. These superintendents reported to the secretary of war, who by 1832 had a commissioner of Indian affairs to handle these matters. When the Department of the Interior was created in 1849, the Bureau of Indian Affairs was transferred to it. As long as the Indians were capable of resistance, the military also had a voice in Indian affairs; there were periods after the Civil War when many army officers were detached for duty as agents.

The fur trade and arable land continued to be prime factors in the Indian problem. Beginning in 1795, the United States maintained a series of trading houses, or factories, among the tribes. Until 1822 these factories supplied goods to the Indians at cost in an attempt to counteract the influence of Spain and England, whose posts the Indians visited in Florida, Louisiana, and Canada.

Not all American interests were served by the factory system. John Jacob Astor of the American Fur Company objected to the competition. Backed by politicians of the caliber of Senator Thomas Hart Benton of Missouri and the long-time governor of the Michigan Territory, Lewis Cass, Astor helped Congress to see the danger to free enterprise posed by the government trading houses. It is probable that Astor also had a hand in an earlier congressional action that had eliminated his Canadian competitors by barring foreigners from the fur trade.

In the 1830s the fur trade began to decline in significance, but Indian land continued to attract speculators and home seekers and to disturb Indian-American relations. Between 1783 and the passage of the Indian Removal Bill in 1830, approximately seventy-five treaties of purchase were negotiated with tribes. The Northwest Ordinance of 1787 had laid down the rule that prior to white occupancy the Indian claims had to be extinguished, but this formality seldom inhibited squatters from staking out claims to choice Indian lands. Army officers and naive government officials trying too strenuously to protect Indian rights were enlightened by politicians pressured by the squatters themselves. If the tribesmen retaliated by destroying surveyors' markers or by scalping an occasional intruder, the expense of the resulting war would be borne by all the people of the United States.

Meanwhile, clashes between state governments and the pockets of Indians left behind as the frontier moved west led to a clearer definition of the Indians' place in American society. The Supreme Court held the tribes to be "domestic dependent nations" under the guardianship of the federal government. In practice, however, Indian interests were always subordinated when they conflicted with those of white voters. Andrew Jackson made this very clear when he declined to back the Supreme Court's decision favoring the Cherokees in their differences with the state of Georgia.

The Indian removal policy flowed from a growing recognition of the incompatibility of the two cultures and the existence of a political system that enfranchised land-hungry settlers but not the Indians whose land the settlers coveted. Rationalized by its architects as a policy benefiting all concerned, it provided for the removal of the Indians to areas west of the Mississippi. There, with troops to isolate them from contamination by unsavory elements among the white frontiersmen, the migrants would be introduced to the refinements of the superior civilization and transformed into peaceful, Christian farmers, while the expanding American population would be developing the fertile acres the Indians had evacuated.

The Indian role in the War of 1812 helped set the stage for the acceptance of the removal policy. Hostile warriors on the frontier had been aided and abetted by the British prior to the declaration of war. The War Hawks of 1812 argued that the seizure of Canada would eliminate this source of danger to the frontier. Such fears were not entirely groundless. At the end of the Revolution one officer in the British Indian service had counseled the Iroquois to surrender their tomahawk, used as a symbol of war, to him. He had promised that he "would not remove it out of sight or far from them, but lay it down carefully by their side, that they might have it convenient to use in defence of their rights and property if they were invaded or molested by the Americans."[6]

Although the British did not deliberately incite the Indians to attack the Americans, the British presence in the Northwest posts as late as 1796 and British gifts to visiting Indian delegations and willingness to hear their tales of woe encouraged the Indians to believe that they had British support. It is likely that without this tacit backing the Indians would not have required three expeditions against them before Anthony Wayne, at the Battle of Fallen Timbers in 1794, ended their resistance for a decade in the Old Northwest. Also, if deprived of British aid and counsel, the Shawnee chief Tecumseh would have been less successful in rallying followers before the War of 1812.

The British represented only part of the problem. A resurgent Spain had regained Florida, and from bases there and in Louisiana the Spanish kept the southeastern tribes in a state of unrest. Southern votes for a declaration of war in 1812 undoubtedly represented a desire to settle the troubles in that quarter by the sword.

In the Old Northwest during the War of 1812 the Indians played their customary roles as auxiliaries, scouts, and raiders for the British forces, keeping the frontier in turmoil. The war actually began for the Indians in the fall of 1811 when they attacked William Henry Harrison, who was threatening their village on Tippecanoe Creek. When the war ended, a joint Indian-British assault on St. Louis was still a distinct possibility in the minds of its nervous citizenry. In the South differences among the Creeks produced a separate war in which that tribe's hostile Red Sticks were crushed by American troops aided by their own Indian allies, including some of the Creeks. The War of 1812 was a disaster for the Indians, but Andrew Jackson and William Henry Harrison emerged from these campaigns with reputations as Indian fighters that would eventually help place them in the White House.

In the two decades after the War of 1812, most of the eastern tribesmen, bewildered and impotent in their defeat, were inveigled into new negotiations, which some of them little understood until they were on their way west. Here and there a tribe chose to resist.

[6]Quoted in Randolph C. Downes, *Council Fires on the Upper Ohio: A Narrative of Indian Affairs on the Upper Ohio until 1795* (Pittsburgh, 1940), 283-84. The officer was Sir John Johnson.

The Sacs and Foxes rallied around the aged Sac warrior Black Hawk when he refused to honor a quarter-century-old treaty of cession negotiated under suspicious circumstances. During intermittent fighting from 1835 to 1842 a remnant of the Seminoles defied the might of the United States from the fastness of the Everglades. But the War of 1812 had terminated the British practice of dabbling in Indian affairs south of the Great Lakes, and Spain no longer operated from Florida. Without outside aid the Indian case was hopeless. Scalps would be lifted on both sides and the taxpayers would provide millions of dollars to pay for these border wars, but the end was never in doubt. By 1860 the Indians were only a memory in most areas east of the Mississippi.

The bedraggled survivors who had migrated west of the river did not prosper according to plan. One veteran agent blamed the whites:

> Our education appears [to the Indians] to consist in knowing how most effectually to cheat them; our civilization in knowing how to pander to the worst propensities of nature, and then beholding the criminal and inhuman results with a cold indifference—a worse than heathen apathy; while our religion is readily summed up in the consideration of dollars and cents.[7]

Despite the best intentions of missionaries subsidized by their denominations and despite teachers and blacksmiths provided by tribal and government funds, the apathetic tribesmen declined shockingly. Faced by new pressures on their lands from the frontiersmen who had followed them across the Mississippi, the Indians consented to being placed on more closely defined reservations, which grew smaller with the successive negotiations. Each of the treaties was justified in terms of the benefits that would accrue for the Indians: they would no longer have surplus land to arouse white cupidity, and the money the Indians would receive in return for the unneeded lands could be used to further their own civilization programs. Sometimes the new treaties required new removals, and the Indians were uprooted once again and shifted to new and strange environments, complicating the civilization process immeasurably. It was useless to tell an Indian who had

[7]John Beach to Governor John Chambers of Iowa, 1 Sept. 1845, 29th Cong., 1st sess., 1845-46, Senate Document no. 1, 485.

been forced to move once, and whose tenure at a new location was uncertain, that he stood to gain by building a house, clearing fields, and planting crops. It was easier to live hand-to-mouth on the small annuities from previous cessions, stalk the little game remaining, and dream of an earlier and happier day when a warrior was not asked to cut his hair, shed his blanket, and do woman's work.

Even the little hunting the warriors did in their new locations presented problems. The concentration of the displaced tribes on the edge of the Plains country was resented by the Indians native to that area. Clashes between the intruders and the natives became frequent, and the buffalo herds upon which both now depended—the Plains Indians entirely and the intruders partially—began to melt away. The Mexican War and settlement of the Oregon question brought new tribes under United States jurisdiction, and with them came new complications of the Indian problem. Concurrently, wagon trains carrying settlers to California and Oregon became a common sight, each taking its toll of the limited grass, timber, and water resources of the area. Moreover, hide hunters slaughtered thousands of buffalo, and the railroads pushing out onto the Plains began to provide the flexibility and speed needed to subjugate the Plains warriors.

Although the Comanches and other Plains Indians were no braver than the typical Eastern Woodland's Mohawk or Shawnee, the Plains Indians' nomadic way of life and abundance of horses made them a more elusive target. Since their acquisition of horses from the Spanish settlers, these Indians had become completely mobile. Unlike the eastern tribes, they had no fixed villages and fields of standing crops to be destroyed. As long as the buffalo herds existed, the Plains Indians had a means of subsistence. With their dependents mounted and all their worldly possessions lashed to horse-drawn travois, these Indians had a sustained rate of march the troopers could not match. Two decades of skirmishing and raiding, highlighted by very few pitched battles, ensued before the disappearance of the buffalo herds and the new mobility given the army by the railroad combined to bring the Indian wars to an end. The romance lingered, and terms like Wagon Box Fight, Adobe Walls, Beecher Island, and the Little Big Horn are still to be reckoned with in American history.

Each of these battles represents a somewhat different facet of the bloodletting on the Plains. The Wagon Box Fight in the summer of 1867 was an incident in the attempt of the United States to keep open the Bozeman Trail, a route from the East to the mining camps in Montana. Troops defeated the Oglala Sioux under Red Cloud in this battle, only one of several in the Sioux semisiege of Fort Phil Kearny, an army strong point on the trail.

During the following summer, southern Plains warriors resisting incarceration on reservations tried to wipe out a small detachment of army scouts on an island in the Arikaree River in western Kansas, an island that now bears the name of one of the victims, Lieutenant F. W. Beecher. Six years later the southern Plains Indians, refusing to adapt to reservation life, were again on the prowl. Their targets this time were the hated hide hunters, and as at Beecher Island and the Wagon Box Fight, the Indian attack at Adobe Walls in 1874 was repelled.

The government's inability to contain its miners, together with unrealistic efforts to metamorphose buffalo Indians into peaceful farmers, set the stage for Custer's demise on the Little Big Horn. The shocking loss of 275 Seventh Cavalry troopers and their dashing commander brought a reevaluation of the policy that could produce such incidents. As long as the fundamental factor in the equation remained—the pressure of the white population on a native people still vigorous and committed to war as a way of life—the bloodshed would continue.

The same situation existed elsewhere, but all the Indians had to be subjugated, including the warlike Navajos and Apaches in the Southwest and the Nez Percés in the Northwest. In the process Geronimo, Cochise, and Chief Joseph became household names in late nineteenth-century America: the Apaches Geronimo and Cochise for campaigns unequaled for ferocity and speed of maneuver, and Chief Joseph for a masterful retreat and chivalric conduct of war that made him the toast of his conquerors. Like the others, those who survived defeat were located on reservations. Alone among the native population, those Indians loosely classified as Pueblos continued their way of life relatively unchanged. In contact with whites since the sixteenth century, the Pueblos' isolation and tightly knit social order ensured their survival.

The Civil War had been an additional catastrophe for the Indians drawn into it. The tribes most severely affected were located in Indian Territory, now Oklahoma. These Indians, themselves once residents of the South and many of their leaders slave owners, had a natural affinity for the Confederacy. As usual, however, unity was lacking. There were Indians of each tribe who either preferred to sit out the war or maintained their allegiance to the United States. This produced further schisms within the tribes involved, and Indian Territory became a no-man's-land, with raiding parties from both sides looting and pilfering. At the conclusion of hostilities some of the tribes who had suffered most were then required, for their support of the Confederacy, to forfeit large areas of land. This, in turn, made possible the removal from Kansas of other Indians, who were relocated on lands extorted from pro-Confederate tribes.

As the Indians' capacity for active resistance declined, there was no corresponding increase in their rate of acculturation. Some critics blamed the practice of recruiting agents from among the ranks of deserving politicians. To substantiate their charges, critics could point to shocking examples of corruption and inefficiency in the Indian service. In response, President Grant inaugurated his Quaker Policy by inviting church groups to nominate Indian agents. This produced considerable bickering among the Christians but did provide some dedicated, if inexperienced, agents. Neither the Quaker Policy nor the abandonment of the unrealistic treaty policy in 1871, however, solved the problem of administration.

Many reformers, who were genuinely concerned with Indian welfare, blamed much of the Indians' lack of progress on three persisting tribal institutions: communal ownership of property, chieftainship, and native religions. Even before the Civil War, occasional treaties made allowance for allotment of land to individual Indians, a practice also known as severalty. Reformers argued that the traditional communal ownership of land deprived individuals of incentive to improve their situations. The reformers envisioned that private property would awaken in the Indians pride of ownership and an acquisitive instinct that would lead them to emulate their white neighbors. As most reservations contained much more land than would be required if the Indians farmed individual allotments, the surplus could be sold to enterprising whites, who would provide a salutary example for the allottees. The proceeds from the sale of the surplus lands then would be applied to schools and other devices designed to speed civilization of the Indians. As a safeguard, during the transition period of twenty-five years the individual Indians would not receive final title to their land.

The first general application of this policy of civilizing through private property was the Dawes Severalty Act of 1887. Only a few Indians, principally the Five Civilized Tribes (as the Cherokees, Creeks, Choctaws, Chickasaws, and Seminoles were known after their removal), were not covered by the Dawes Act; subsequent legislation applied the policy to them. Briefly, the Dawes Act provided that the president, at his discretion, could allot reservation land to individual Indians. After a twenty-five year delay to allow the Indian to grow into his new responsibilities, the warrior-turned-farmer would receive final title to his land and U.S. citizenship. Any land remaining after allotment would be sold to whites and the proceeds applied to civilizing the allottees. Certainly no policy was ever implemented with greater confidence in its success than the severalty program. The opinion of Henry Knox, Washington's secretary of war, had been echoed for a century: "Were it possible to introduce among the... tribes a love for exclusive property,"[8] civilization of the Indians would quickly follow.

Chieftainship, which reformers saw as the second stumbling block in the Indians' path, had once been encouraged among the tribes by government officials. Chiefs were then regarded as a convenient means of contact and control. As the problem of control became less important, chiefs came to be considered as vestigial remnants of barbarism that should be eliminated. Chiefs were now bypassed, and government agents chose to deal with the tribes through councils elected by the tribesmen or selected from the more amenable headmen. As a further means of undercutting the chiefs, maintenance of law and order was delegated to newly created tribal police forces and Courts of Indian Offenses.

The third institution attacked by reformers was native religion,

[8]Knox to President Washington, 7 July 1789, *American State Papers: Indian Affairs* (Washington, 1832-34), 1: 53.

which buttressed the positions of many Indian chiefs. The practice of native religions was discouraged, some ceremonies were actually forbidden, and Christian missionaries were encouraged. Particularly distressing and alarming to Indian service personnel was the appearance of the Indian prophets, men like Wovoka of the Paiute and Smoholla of the Sokulk. Comparable to the earlier Delaware Prophet, who had provided spiritual backing for Pontiac's resistance movement, the new Indian prophets saw visions of a return to the good old days when the Plains were uncontaminated by whites and swarming with buffalo herds. These testimonials had frightening overtones of violence for white officials. One of the last instances of the employment of troops against Indians, the Wounded Knee Massacre of 1890, stemmed from a situation created by the Ghost Dance among the Sioux. With the buffalo gone and the Sioux under the eyes of troops armed with artillery and Gatling guns, even the gods failed the Indians.

While communal ownership of property, chieftainship, and native religions came under attack, efforts were made to educate a new generation of Indians at private and government schools. The off-reservation boarding school was considered the ideal agency for the indoctrination of young Indians with the virtues of the white man's way of life. There the students could be isolated from the corrupting influences of their native environment. At the Carlisle Indian School, Captain Richard H. Pratt carried this one step further by using an "outing" system, which placed the Indian youths with white families for extended periods of time.

Though the reformers moved with great optimism, the returns from these programs were most disappointing to the friends of the Indian. Severalty did not inspire the hunter to become a self-sufficient farmer; severalty made it easier to relieve the Indian of many valuable acres to the satisfaction of the white population of western states. By 1934 approximately two-thirds of the land held by the Indians in 1887, including much of their best land, had passed into white hands. The earnest efforts of missionaries did not spark any wholesale conversion to Christianity. The Indians did, however, incorporate some elements of Christianity into new religious cults such as the Native American Church, which used peyote in its ritual. The education programs were likewise a disappointment. They most frequently produced boys and girls caught between two cultures, scorned and rejected by the conservatives among their own people and unable to function anywhere but on the fringes of white society. Only in the destruction of the power of the chiefs did the government agents enjoy much success, and there they only created a vacuum of power to be occupied by individuals sometimes more grasping and less concerned with Indian welfare than those they had supplanted.

As tribal populations continued to decline in the first quarter of the twentieth century, the Indian indeed appeared to be the "Vanishing American." In addition, the policies pursued by the government up to the mid-1920s were essentially those designed to achieve assimilation, but which had been most successful in separating the Indians from their land.

By 1933 the bankruptcy of these policies was apparent to all who took the trouble to examine them, and new programs emerged during the administration of newly elected President Franklin D. Roosevelt. As part of the Indian New Deal, the allotment policy was ended and the tribes were encouraged to acquire land and engage in business enterprises. Tribal self-government was fostered and new respect was accorded tribal cultures. Commissioner of Indian Affairs John Collier believed that a tribal existence was appropriate for Indians, and the government's pressures for assimilation were sharply reduced.

The pendulum began to swing back in the 1940s, and the special Indian-United States relationship became a target for those seeking to reduce the scale of government expenditures. Severing the official ties that tribes had with the government became the order of the day. This termination policy was pursued until the early 1960s, although few tribes actually lost their special status as wards of the United States. Concurrently, the government embarked on a relocation program by which thousands of Indians were encouraged to leave their reservations and seek new lives in urban areas.

The administrations of John F. Kennedy, Lyndon B. Johnson, and Richard M. Nixon saw a transition to new policies. Relocation was soft-pedaled, and the new emphasis was on creating jobs on the reservations by attracting light industry and fostering tourism. The new slogan was "self-determination," which called for the Indians to be freed of government controls while retaining government financial support. Federal aid to reservations increased measurably in the 1960s and 1970s. Nevertheless, the Indian homelands continued to be plagued by high unemployment and mortality rates and some of the lowest standards of living in the nation. It was also doubtful that traditional tribal lifestyles could accommodate themselves to the manpower needs of industry and tourism.

Another shift in government policy became apparent in the early 1980s as President Ronald Reagan attempted to reduce the level of government domestic spending. This did not bode well for the maintenance of the approximately seventy federal programs that provided the sources of funds for tribal operations.

The Indians, however, guided by a new generation of college-trained leaders and supported by treasuries fattened by court judgments, fought to retain their slice of the federal pie. One by-product of termination had been the government's effort to prepare Indians for termination by permitting them to seek the settlement of old claims against the United States. That had resulted in the creation of the Indian Claims Commission, which awarded tribes judgments totalling over half a billion dollars. Most of that money had been distributed in per capita payments, but tribal treasuries benefited as well.

The announcements of multimillion-dollar judgments prompted tribal members who had drifted from the reservations to reassert their Indian identity. Eastern tribes experienced a similar resurgence in population after the success of the Penobscot and Passamaquoddy in securing a lucrative settlement of their claim that they had been deprived of land in clear violation of the provisions of the 1790 Indian Intercourse Act.

The census of 1980 revealed that 1.4 million Americans identified themselves as Indians, as opposed to only 800,000 in 1970. Clearly the work of the Indian Claims Commission and the possibility of awards for eastern tribes were factors in this increase, but there were other explanations. The federal programs available to individual Indians and tribes had made Indian identity more financially attractive in the 1970s. Also, new respect was being accorded to Indians, who were now lauded as the first conservationists, a people who lived in harmony with nature.

Probably the most important factor in the new pride in "Indianness" was the Red Power movement launched in the 1960s.

Indian activists began to attract attention in the media by a wave of demonstrations, the most notable of which were the seizure of Alcatraz Island and the occupation of Wounded Knee. It is significant that the leadership for these activities came not from the elected tribal leaders, but from the younger, more militant, and usually nonreservation Indians.

The increased interest in Indian identity, both for psychological and financial reasons, has reawakened concern for the problem of identifying who is an Indian. Being on the roll of a tribe recognized by the federal government is the only sure means of legal acceptance as an Indian. Such acknowledged tribes are also the only ones certain of eligibility for federal aid programs. The success of the Menominee of Wisconsin in reversing termination, and of the Penobscot and Passamaquoddy of Maine and the Western Pequot of Connecticut in securing federal recognition, inspired about a hundred other tribes to seek such status.

At least one thing has not changed: the amazing diversity of the individuals and groups designated as Native American. Native Americans include members of a tribe with a population of over 150,000 and a huge reservation rich in mineral deposits. More typically, the Indian belongs to a tribe of fewer than 4,000 members with a land base inadequate for the tribal sovereignty that has become an Indian rallying cry in the late twentieth century. To formulate policies for such a variety of peoples is as difficult today as it was when President Thomas Jefferson devoted so much of his time and energy to the Indian question. Today, however, the Indians do not play the role in international relations that they did when Jefferson occupied the White House. No longer holding the balance of power between nations contending for control of North America, the Indian for most Americans is simply a figure of history. Nevertheless, a study of the Indians and their fellows and the wide range of cultures they represent is rewarding to any student of humanity. Moreover, if we are to understand American history and the Jeffersons and Tecumsehs who made it, as well as the evolution of American aspirations as a people over the centuries, there is no better subject for study than U.S. relations with the Native Americans.

SUGGESTIONS FOR FURTHER READING

The thirteen years since the last revision of this pamphlet have seen a remarkable flowering of Indian studies as a new generation of scholars, attracted to the field in the late 1960s and early 1970s, begin to make their mark. This is not simply a matter of quantity. Both the older practitioners and the recent entrants to the field have been sensitized to the need to try to get more "Indian" into their Indian history, to try to write more from within. Nevertheless, most of the history being written continues to fall into the same categories, tribal histories or studies of government policies and programs, which are based overwhelmingly on documentation prepared by whites and preserved in archives created and administered by whites.

In selecting the items to be included in this brief bibliography, the principal criteria have been to meet the needs of the newcomer to the field and of the teacher desiring to enrich a course with additional Indian materials. For those wishing to pursue a topic further, there is a fine bibliography available, Francis Paul Prucha, *A Bibliographical Guide to the History of Indian-White Relations in the United States* (Chicago, 1977), with a supplement, *Indian-White Relations in the United States: A Bibliography of Works Published 1975-1980* (Lincoln, 1982).

The best one-volume survey of Indian culture continues to be Harold E. Driver, *Indians of North America* (Chicago, 1969). The old *Handbook of American Indians North of Mexico* (Washington, 1907; reprint, New York, 1959) is being replaced by the Smithsonian Institution's multivolume *Handbook of North American Indians,* whose general editor is William C. Sturtevant. Five volumes have been published (one each for the Northeast, California, and the Subarctic; two on the Southwest), and twelve others are in process. The series deals with the culture, history, and current condition of the Indians and is an invaluable reference work.

Ruth M. Underhill, *Red Man's Religion* (Chicago, 1965), remains the best survey of that vital element in Indian life. For the role of the supernatural in a single tribe, see Peter J. Powell, *Sweet Medicine* (Norman, 1969), a study of the religious practices of the Northern Cheyenne by an Anglo-Catholic priest with a rare appreciation for that people's faith.

On a related topic, medical practices, Virgil J. Vogel, *American Indian Medicine* (Norman, 1970), is the authority. Vogel emphasizes the use of indigenous botanical drugs rather than the curing ceremonies that so often attract the observer.

For Indian arts and crafts, a good survey is Julia M. Seton, *American Indian Arts* (New York, 1962). It covers such topics as music, dance, basketry, weaving, bead and quill work, and pottery. An important art form is covered in more detail in Margery Bedinger, *Indian Silver: Navajo and Pueblo Jewelers* (Albuquerque, 1973).

Several general studies of Indian-white relations are available. A very useful volume, designed as a text for courses in Indian history, is Arrell Morgan Gibson, *The American Indian: Prehistory to the Present* (Lexington, Mass., 1980). Wilcomb E. Washburn, *The Indian in America* (New York, 1975), is particularly good on the seventeenth and eighteenth centuries and smoothly integrates anthropology and history. William T. Hagan, *American Indians* (Chicago, 1979), is a brief survey emphasizing the policies of the government during the different historical periods. For important acts of Congress, court decisions, and statements of policy by government officials, a convenient collection is Francis Paul Prucha, ed., *Documents of United States Indian Policy* (Lincoln, 1975).

Those wishing to examine the views of Indians held by Americans throughout their history, views that helped determine actions of government, can consult Robert F. Berkhofer, Jr., *The White Man's Indian: Images of the American Indian from Columbus to the Present* (New York, 1978).

A very important element in government programs for Indians has been education. Evelyn C. Adams, *American Indian Education* (New York, 1946), is still useful. Francis Paul Prucha, *The Churches and the Indian Schools, 1888-1912* (Lincoln, 1979), highlights the efforts of Catholic educators to secure equal treatment for their extensive operations on the reservations. Margaret Szasz, *Education and the American Indian* (Albuquerque, 1974), is indispensable for federal policy in the twentieth century.

One approach to Indian history is through biography. Frederick J. Dockstader, *Great North American Indians* (New York, 1977), profiles three hundred important individuals. R. David Edmunds, ed., *American Indian Leaders* (Lincoln, 1980), provides chapters on some of the most significant individuals: Old Briton, Joseph Brant, Alexander McGillivray, Red Bird, John Ross, Satanta, Washakie, Sitting Bull, Quanah Parker, Dennis Bushyhead, Carlos Montezuma, and Peter MacDonald. Later in this essay references are made to book-length biographies in connection with discussion of the periods in which the individuals lived.

The important role of missionaries from earliest times to the present is chronicled in Henry Warner Bowden, *American Indians and Christian Missions: Studies in Cultural Conflict* (Chicago, 1981). The subtitle suggests Bowden's recognition of the persisting importance of native beliefs. Other authorities on this topic are Robert F. Berkhofer, Jr. and R. Pierce Beaver. Berkhofer's *Salvation and the Savage* (Lexington, Ky., 1965) is confined to the period between 1787 and 1862, while Beaver's *Church, State, and the American Indian* (St. Louis, 1966) surveys Protestant activity from the colonial period to the 1870s. The work of Catholic missionaries in a particular area is handled competently in Robert Ignatius Burns, S.J., *The Jesuits and the Indian Wars of the Northwest* (New Haven, 1966), which has a broader coverage than the title suggests.

The key officials in the government's relations with the Indians were the agents. Usually political appointees and completely unprepared for their responsibilities, these agents compiled a mixed record. The subjects of Flora Warren Seymour, *Indian Agents of the Old Frontier* (New York, 1941), are drawn largely from the second half of the nineteenth century. They include such well-known figures as Alfred B. Meacham, James McLaughlin, and Valentine T. McGillycuddy. Two reprints that shed further light on the life of the Indian agent are Lawrie Tatum, *Our Red Brothers* (Lincoln, 1970), and E. E. White, *Experiences of a Special Indian Agent* (Norman, 1965). Tatum, one of the Quaker agents appointed during the Grant administration, served for three years on the Kiowa, Comanche, and Kiowa-Apache Reservation. As a special agent, White served with these Indians and others. The two books together give a sampling of the problems associated with administering a reservation.

Fur trappers and traders encountered the Indians even before the agents. For the best picture of the attitudes of fur traders toward Indians, see Lewis O. Saum, *The Fur Trader and the Indian*

(Seattle, 1965). Sylvia Van Kirk has a very interesting account of Indian and mixed-blood women involved in some fashion with the fur trade and fur traders of Canada. Many of the conclusions drawn in her study, *Many Tender Ties: Women in Fur Trade Society* (Norman, 1983), are applicable to the trade in the United States. The most controversial book relating to Indians and the fur trade is Calvin Martin, *Keepers of the Game: Indian-Animal Relationships and the Fur Trade* (Berkeley, 1978), and should be read in conjunction with *Indians, Animals, and the Fur Trade: A Critique of Keepers of the Game* (Athens, 1981), edited by Shepard Krech III. Martin advanced the provocative thesis that some Indians blamed the animals for the terrible losses the Indians had suffered from the diseases imported by Europeans, and in a spirit of revenge slaughtered game far beyond Indian needs for the fur trade.

On the colonial period of Indian-white relations there are several important studies. Douglas Edward Leach, *Flintlock and Tomahawk: New England in King Philip's War* (New York, 1958), is the best military treatment of the war that broke the back of Indian resistance in that area. Alden T. Vaughan, *New England Frontier: Puritans and Indians, 1620-1675* (Boston, 1965), is a defense of the Puritans against charges that they were racists who trampled on Indian rights. In turn, this view has been rejected by Francis Jennings, *The Invasion of America: Indians, Colonialism, and the Cant of Conquest* (Chapel Hill, 1975), and Neal Salisbury, *Manitou and Providence: Indians, Europeans, and the Making of New England, 1500-1643* (New York, 1982). Jennings is particularly scathing in his denunciation of the Puritans and their defenders. In his own study, Salisbury shares Jennings's view of the Puritans and includes a fine overview of the life of the New England tribes before the invasion of the Europeans.

In New York the powerful Iroquois Confederacy played a major role in the colonial period. The relations of the Iroquois in the seventeenth century with the English, French, and Dutch are portrayed in Allen W. Trelease, *Indian Affairs in Colonial New York* (Ithaca, 1960). Georgiana C. Nammack's slim volume, *Fraud, Politics, and the Dispossession of the Indians* (Norman, 1969), investigates four specific cases in which the Iroquois were defrauded of land, experiences that poisoned their relations with the colonists and help explain Iroquois support of George III during the Revolution. Francis Jennings, *The Ambiguous Empire: The Covenant Chain Confederation of Indian Tribes with English Colonies from Its Beginnings to the Lancaster Treaty of 1774* (New York, 1984), highlights diplomacy and argues that talk of an Iroquois empire was a device by which the British, as the Iroquois overlords, could claim more of North America in the contest with the French. Richard Aquila, *The Iroquois Restoration: Iroquois Diplomacy on the Colonial Frontier, 1701-1754* (Detroit, 1983), also stresses means other than warfare by which the confederation maintained its position.

The Iroquois played a significant role in the American Revolution, as is revealed by Barbara Graymont's very able *The Iroquois and the American Revolution* (Syracuse, 1972). For the career of the best known Iroquois leader during and after the Revolution, see Barbara Thompson Kelsey, *Joseph Brant 1743-1807* (Syracuse, 1984). It is a lengthy biography of an Indian who did his best to protect his people's interests against the machinations of both the British and the Americans. One Iroquois tribe with which Brant had little influence was the Seneca. In *The Death and Rebirth of the Seneca* (New York, 1970), Anthony F. C. Wallace provided an excellent picture of this largest of the Iroquois tribes during its decline in the late colonial period and subsequent revitalization under religious leader Handsome Lake.

For the history of the southern tribes during the colonial period, the best survey is J. Leitch Wright, Jr., *The Only Land They Knew: The Tragic Story of the American Indians of the Old South* (New York, 1981). Wright is particularly interested in Indians as slaves and slave owners. James H. O'Donnell III, *Southern Indians in the American Revolution* (Knoxville, 1973), presents a concise discussion of this important subject.

In the years 1755 to 1795 the upper Ohio Valley was a key frontier region. A good picture of what transpired there is found in Randolph C. Downes, *Council Fires on the Upper Ohio* (Pittsburgh, 1940). Downes begins with the English and French competition for Indian trade and support in the French and Indian War, carries the discussion through the Revolution, and briefly sketches developments to the mid-1790s.

R. David Edmunds is the author of three studies that together provide an excellent appreciation for what was happening to the tribes between the Ohio and Mississippi rivers. *The Potawatomis* (Norman, 1978) traces the history of that tribe from its first alliances with the French and participation in the colonial wars to the removal of the main body of the tribe to Kansas in 1840. Edmunds's *Tecumseh* (Boston, 1984) and *The Shawnee Prophet* (Lincoln, 1983) relate the careers of the two brothers who created an intertribal confederacy to try to stay the American advance. Edmunds argues persuasively that the Prophet initiated the confederacy with his religious revitalization program, but that Tecumseh better fit the white man's idea of an Indian leader and thus has fared better with the historians.

For government policy in the early national period, a good starting point is Francis Paul Prucha, *American Indian Policy in the Formative Years: The Indian Trade and Intercourse Acts 1790-1834* (Cambridge, 1962). This can be supplemented by Herman J. Viola, *Thomas L. McKenney: Architect of America's Early Indian Policy, 1816-1830* (Chicago, 1974), and Ronald N. Satz, *American Indian Policy in the Jacksonian Era* (Lincoln, 1975). McKenney headed both the office of Indian trade and the forerunner of the Bureau of Indian Affairs; he was a major force in shaping the Indian Removal Act of 1830. Satz's volume is a dispassionate discussion of the origins of removal; the book is no less damning for the absence of emotion. Equally effective is Satz's portrayal of the rapid and uncoordinated growth of the federal bureaucracy that arose to service the scores of tribes with close ties to the government.

The presentation of Indian removal has been largely in terms of the Five Civilized Tribes, although it was an experience that befell many others. A good popular account of the Cherokee Trail of Tears and the events that led up to it is Samuel Carter III, *Cherokee Sunset, A Nation Betrayed* (Garden City, 1976). For the life of the Cherokee chief who played a major role in his tribe's affairs from the 1820s to the 1860s, see Gary E. Moulton, *John Ross* (Athens, 1978). Arthur H. DeRosier, Jr., *The Removal of the Choctaw Indians* (Knoxville, 1970), and Michael D. Green, *The Politics of Removal: Creek Government and Society in Crisis* (Lincoln, 1982), help fill out the picture of removal. The underlying motive for removal—land acquisition by the United States—is the subject of a sophisticated study, Mary Elizabeth Young, *Redskins, Ruffleshirts, and Rednecks* (Norman, 1962). Young is primarily concerned with the fraud and chicanery involved in the government's purchases of land from the Creeks, Choctaws, and Chickasaws. The most recent effort to summarize the complicated wars in which the Seminoles resisted efforts to move them west is Virginia Bergman Peters, *The Florida Wars* (Hamden, Conn., 1979). Francis Paul Prucha, *The Sword of the Republic* (New York, 1969), is a well-rounded account of all of the Indian wars between 1783 and 1846.

Although the removal of the Indians from the Middle West has received less attention, there are some useful accounts. R. David Edmunds's previously cited history of the Potawatomis covers their removal. Black Hawk's story is unique as an autobiography of an Indian who opposed his tribe's ouster and in the process brought on an Indian war. Although the autobiography bears the mark of the white translator, it reveals the spirit of the Indian patriot who chose resistance over accommodation. The best edition is Donald Jackson, *Ma-ka-tai-me-she-kia-kiak, Black Hawk: An Autobiography* (Urbana, 1955). For the circumstances that produced the Black Hawk War and the fate of the tribes involved, see William T. Hagan, *The Sac and Fox Indians* (Norman, 1958).

A remarkably successful synthesis of the history and culture of the Indians of the Southwest is Edward H. Spicer, *Cycles of Conquest: The Impact of Spain, Mexico, and the United States on the Indians of the Southwest, 1533-1960* (Tucson, 1962). George Howard Phillips, *Chiefs and Challengers: Indian Resistance and Cooperation in Southern California* (Berkeley, 1975), recounts the experience of three California tribes with the Spanish, Mexican, and American invaders.

Given the importance of the topic and the availability of the documents, it is understandable that government policy has attracted the attention of numerous scholars. Robert A. Trennert, Jr., *Alternative to Extinction: Federal Indian Policy and the Beginnings of the Reservation System, 1846-1851* (Philadelphia, 1975), helps set the stage for what came later. His *Indian Traders on the Middle Border: The House of Ewing, 1827-54* (Lincoln, 1981) illustrates clearly the fundamental influence traders could have on the implementation of Indian policy, an influence that too often has gone unreported.

For the Civil War and post-Civil War period, several works are available. David A. Nichols, *Lincoln and the Indians: Civil War*

Policy and Politics (Columbia, 1978), is better on the politics than the policy. Robert H. Keller, *American Protestantism and United States Indian Policy, 1869-1882* (Lincoln, 1983), is the most recent study of the Ulysses S. Grant administration's efforts to employ on reservations individuals recommended by churches and to replace military operations by diplomacy in dealing with the Plains tribes. A dependable account of the Native American whom President Grant appointed commissioner of Indian affairs is William H. Armstrong, *Warrior in Two Camps: Ely S. Parker, Union General and Seneca Chief* (Syracuse, 1978). The best source for the role of reformers in shaping Indian policy in the late nineteenth century is Francis Paul Prucha, *American Indian Policy in Crisis: Christian Reformers and the Indian, 1865-1890* (Norman, 1976).

Frequently, there was quite a gulf between the policy the reformers helped to shape and what actually transpired on the reservations. This is amply demonstrated in two books. Clyde A. Milner II, *With Good Intentions: Quaker Work among the Pawnees, Otos, and Omahas* (Lincoln, 1982), analyzes the conduct of members of that religious group who were appointed to positions on reservations by President Grant. Milner concludes that the problems that native societies confronted in this period defied solution by even the best-intentioned administrators. H. Craig Miner and William E. Unrau, *The End of Indian Kansas* (Lawrence, 1978), details how tribes that had been removed to Kansas were shifted from that state or coerced into selling most of their land. It is a sordid story of venal white officials and incompetent and sometimes corrupt Indian leaders. The same might be said of Angie Debo, *And Still the Waters Run* (Princeton, 1940), which documents to a degree uncomfortable to the white reader the cavalier treatment accorded the rights and property of the Five Civilized Tribes from the 1890s into the 1930s.

A valuable and unique study that has broader concerns than the impact of government policy is Richard White, *The Roots of Dependency: Subsistence, Environment, and Social Change among the Choctaws, Pawnees, and Navajos* (Lincoln, 1983). White describes how forces that these Indians could not control destroyed the independence of these peoples, who represented three aboriginal subsistence systems.

There are many tribal studies; hardly a major group has been ignored, and now several of the minor ones have attracted the attention of scholars. The following is only a sampling of those available. John C. Ewers, *The Blackfeet* (Norman, 1958), set the standard for others to follow by effectively combining a history of a tribe with an analysis of its culture. Roy W. Meyer, *History of the Santee Sioux* (Lincoln, 1967), is about those Indians best known for their bloody uprising in 1862. He also is the author of *The Village Indians of the Upper Missouri: The Mandans, Hidatsas, and Arikaras* (Lincoln, 1977), a well-executed account of village dwellers contacted early by the fur traders. The Chippewas likewise were early targets of the traders and later of the lumbermen. For the story of some of them, see Edmund Jefferson Danziger, Jr., *The Chippewas of Lake Superior* (Norman, 1978).

Northern Plains tribes have been conspicuous in the history of Indian-white relations. James C. Olson, *Red Cloud and the Sioux Problem* (Lincoln, 1965), depicts a celebrated Oglala chief and his people. One of the most tragic episodes in the life of the Sioux was the Ghost Dance uprising, the subject of Robert M. Utley, *The Last Days of the Sioux Nation* (New Haven, 1963). Northern Cheyenne neighbors of the Sioux have been fortunate to have as their historian Father Peter John Powell, author of *People of the Sacred Mountain* (San Francisco, 1981). Powell has for years been a student of Cheyenne history and culture and presents the Cheyenne version of their past.

The Southern Cheyennes have found a more conventional but no less able historian in Donald J. Berthrong. His *Southern Cheyennes* (Norman, 1963) and *The Cheyenne and Arapaho Ordeal: Reservation and Agency Life in the Indian Territory, 1875-1907* (Norman, 1976) cover their history from pre-reservation times into the twentieth century.

Many of the tribes that had been moved from other regions to Indian Territory also have been the subject of histories. Among the best of these is Arrell M. Gibson, *The Chickasaws* (Norman, 1980). Another tribe that has been well served is the Quapaws. The movement of this small group from their ancestral home in the Arkansas River Valley to Indian Territory and their travail there is traced in W. David Baird, *The Quapaws* (Norman, 1980). William E. Unrau, *The Kansa Indians: A History of the Wind People, 1673-1873* (Norman, 1971), is about a tribe with a similar experience.

Some Indians forcibly resisted removal to reservations. The best single volume on the wars that ensued is Robert M. Utley, *The Indian Frontier of the American West, 1846-1890* (Albuquerque, 1984), which has a full bibliography facilitating further investigation of particular conflicts. In all of these wars, Indians served with the United States Army as scouts and auxiliaries, and their story is told in Thomas W. Dunlay, *Wolves for the Blue Soldiers* (Lincoln, 1982). Apaches resisted American pressure the longest, and the careers of two of their most celebrated leaders are available in Dan L. Thrapp, *Victorio and the Mimbres Apaches* (Norman, 1974), and Angie Debo, *Geronimo* (Norman, 1976). An Indian view of the most celebrated battle of all, Custer's defeat, can be read in John Stands In Timber and Margot Liberty, *Cheyenne Memories* (New Haven, 1967), which is a Cheyenne's version of his tribe's history.

The Jicarilla Apaches and the Navajos gave up armed resistance relatively early. Veronica E. Velarde Tiller, herself a member of the tribe, is the author of the able *The Jicarilla Apache Tribe* (Lincoln, 1983). After the invasion of their homeland by an army column led by Colonel Kit Carson, most of the Navajos were subjected to the "Long Walk." What was at the end of the "Long Walk" is the subject of Gerald Thompson, *The Army and the Navajo: The Bosque Redondo Reservation Experiment, 1863-1868* (Tucson, 1976). With the Bosque Redondo ordeal behind them, the Navajos returned to their homeland. In the following years white traders played an increasingly important role in the lives of the Navajos; some traders made a substantial contribution by fostering and influencing Navajo crafts. This important topic is discussed in Frank McNitt, *The Indian Traders* (Norman, 1962).

To the north and west of the Navajos dozens of other tribes were being subjected to the reservation experience. Gae Whitney Canfield, *Sarah Winnemucca of the Northern Paiutes* (Norman, 1983), examines an Indian woman who defied both Indian and white concepts of a woman's role to exercise leadership among her people in their early reservation period. The best treatment of the tribe whose most celebrated member was Chief Joseph is Alvin M. Josephy, Jr., *The Nez Perce Indians and the Opening of the Northwest* (New Haven, 1965). Robert H. Ruby and John A. Brown have collaborated on histories of two tribes of the Pacific Northwest, *The Cayuse Indians: Imperial Tribesmen of Old*

Oregon (Norman, 1972) and *The Chinook Indians: Traders of the Lower Columbia River* (Norman, 1976).

In the twentieth century something approaching national Indian movements first appeared. Hazel W. Hertzberg, *The Search for an American Indian Identity: Modern Pan-Indian Movements* (Syracuse, 1971), traces the efforts of several national Indian groups. Two individuals who figure prominently in Hertzberg's narrative are themselves subjects of sound biographies: Raymond Wilson, *Ohiyesa: Charles Eastman, Santee Sioux* (Urbana, 1983), and Peter Iverson, *Carlos Montezuma and the Changing World of American Indians* (Albuquerque, 1982).

On the opposition of a leading white reformer to government policy in the 1920s, an excellent source is Lawrence C. Kelly, *The Assault on Assimilation: John Collier and the Origins of Indian Policy Reform* (Albuquerque, 1983). Appointed commissioner of Indian affairs in 1933 by President Franklin D. Roosevelt, Collier undertook sweeping changes in policy. Historians have tended to be critical of Collier, as can be seen in Kenneth R. Philp, *John Collier's Crusade for Indian Reform, 1920-1954* (Tucson, 1971), and Graham D. Taylor, *The New Deal and American Indian Tribalism: The Administration of the Indian Reorganization Act, 1934-45* (Lincoln, 1980).

Fortunately, a few historians have chosen to focus on the impact of the Indian New Deal on particular tribes. Donald L. Parman, *The Navajos and the New Deal* (New Haven, 1976), is a competent study of the nation's largest tribe during that critical period. It can be supplemented by Peter Iverson, *The Navajo Nation* (Westport, Conn., 1981), which is devoted principally to events in the twentieth century. Laurence M. Hauptman, *The Iroquois and the New Deal* (Syracuse, 1981), is a successful effort to evaluate the reactions of Iroquois in three states—New York, Wisconsin, and Oklahoma—to Collier's reforms. An Iroquois (Tuscarora) whose life spanned the emergence of Indian activism in this century was Clinton Rickard. His autobiography, *Fighting Tuscarora* (Syracuse, 1973), edited by Barbara Graymont, is particularly valuable for Rickard's participation in the United States-Canadian border-crossing disputes. (Iroquois were located on both sides of the international boundary.)

The Indian New Deal was followed by an effort to terminate the special relationship tribes had with the government. The only volume devoted entirely to the policy of that period is Larry W. Burt, *Tribalism in Crisis: Federal Indian Policy, 1953-1961* (Albuquerque, 1982). The tribe whose experience was most publicized is the subject of Nicholas C. Peroff, *Menominee Drums: Tribal Termination and Restoration, 1954-1974* (Norman, 1982). In the same time period, some Sioux Indians were displaced by the construction of dams and reservoirs. Michael L. Lawson, *Damned Indians: The Pick-Sloan Plan and the Missouri River Sioux, 1944-1980* (Norman, 1982), describes the trauma this displacement produced.

The mood of Indian activists who opposed termination and went on to launch the Red Power movement is sketched in Stan Steiner, *The New Indians* (New York, 1968). An Indian intellectual whose writing is enlivened by his biting wit is Vine Deloria, Jr. His *Custer Died for Your Sins* (New York, 1969) covers some of the same ground as *The New Indians,* but from the vantage point of an individual who for three years headed the most important national Indian organization. Alvin M. Josephy, Jr., *Red Power* (New York, 1971), is a selection of statements by Indian activists, as well as other material that is useful for an understanding of the objectives of the movement and the conditions that produced it. Josephy's *Now That the Buffalo's Gone* (New York, 1982) is an effort to establish the present status of the Indians by recounting the historical experience of seven groups. His chapter on the Sioux contains a sympathetic version of the American Indian movement's struggle to control the Pine Ridge Reservation, a struggle that brought on the siege of Wounded Knee in 1973.

DCP3/85 1.5M

Augsburg College
George Sverdrup Library
Minneapolis, MN 55454
WITHDRAWN